Mini Amigurumi

SARA SCALES

Mini Amigurumi

THE GUILD OF MASTER CRAFTSMAN
PUBLICATIONS

First published 2013 by
Guild of Master Craftsman Publications Ltd
Castle Place, 166 High Street,
Lewes, East Sussex, BN7 1XU

ISBN 978-1-86108-965-6

A catalogue record for this book is available from
the British Library.

Publisher Jonathan Bailey
Production Manager Jim Bulley
Managing Editor Gerrie Purcell
Senior Project Editor Virginia Brehaut
Copy Editor Judith Chamberlain-Webber
Managing Art Editor Gilda Pacitti
Design Chloë Alexander
Pattern Checker Jude Roust
Photographers Laurel Guilfoyle and Anthony Bailey

Set in Gill Sans

Colour origination by GMC Reprographics
Printed and bound in China

Why we love mini Amigurumi

As a miniaturist, I am always on the lookout for the next item I can shrink – so when crochet came into my life about five years ago, it was obvious where it would end up. My first love with crochet is the art of Amigurumi; with its cute designs and simple techniques, it is a must for any beginner to try.

It was not long before I decided to shrink my Amigurumi work down to what I like to call 'minigurumi'. At first it takes a bit of patience; you also need good eyesight, good glasses or a magnifier if you feel it is needed. Your patience will pay off though, as soon as you see your little creation come to life.

Originally my little characters and trinkets were designed for the dolls' house arena, but increasingly friends and family started to ask me to make them into jewellery items and general gifts. This led me to rethink and experiment with some novelty ideas.

I am not an expert in jewellery-making, so my techniques are simple and at a level that anyone can achieve. By using basic accessories, you can turn your mini Amigurumi into a perfect gift – all you need is a little bit of imagination.

Now it is over to you – don't forget the most important thing is to enjoy, relax and love what you are doing.

Sara Scales

Contents

This cute bird reminded me of a character from one of my son's favourite television shows. Make this chirpy little chap for any bird-lovers you know.

Little bird

Finished size

Approx. ¾ x ¾in (2 x 2cm)

Materials

Anchor Pearl Cotton No 8, 100% cotton
   (89yd/81m per 10g ball)
1 x 10g ball of 128 light blue (A)
1 x 10g ball of 410 dark blue (B)
1 x 10g ball of 305 yellow (C)
1.00mm (UK4:US10) crochet hook

Toy stuffing
2 black seed beads
Beading needle
Large sewing needle
Black embroidery thread
Embroidery needle

Body

Round 1: Using A, create a slip knot, ch 2.

Round 2: 6 dc into first ch.

Round 3: 2 dc into each dc (12 sts).

Round 4: (1 dc in next dc, dc2inc), rep 6 times (18 sts).

Round 5: (Dc in next 2 dc, dc2inc), rep 6 times (24 sts).

Rounds 6–11: Dc around.

Round 12: (Dc in next 2 dc, dc2tog), rep 6 times (18 sts).

Round 13: Dc around.

Round 14: (1 dc in next dc, dc2tog), rep 6 times (12 sts).

Stuff item.

Round 15: Dc2tog around until the hole is closed.

Fasten off.

Break yarn, leaving approximately a 6in (15cm) tail.

Thread the yarn tail through a large sewing needle. Close any gap left at the top then thread the remainder through the body of the bird, and trim.

Wings (make 2)

Round 1: Using B, create a slip knot, ch 2.

Round 2: 6 dc into first ch.

Round 3: 2 dc into each dc (12 sts).

Fasten off.

Break yarn, leaving approximately a 6in (15cm) tail.

Feet (make 2)

Round 1: Using C, create a slip knot, ch 2.

Round 2: 6 dc into first ch.

Fasten off.

Break yarn, leaving approximately a 6in (15cm) tail.

Tail

Row 1: Using B, create a slip knot, ch 2.

Row 2: 1 dc into first ch, turn.

Row 3: Ch 3, (2 tr, 1 ch, 3 tr) into same dc, turn.

Row 4: Ch 3, 1 tr in each st.

Fasten off.

Break yarn, leaving approximately a 6in (15cm) tail.

Making up

Using the yarn tails attached to the separate pieces, stitch the wings, feet and tail into place using mattress stitch (see page 140). Embroider the beak using shade C, by making two French knots on top of each other so they stick out (see page 141). Using the embroidery thread and backstitch (see page 140), stitch on the eyes. Create a tuft using the embroidery thread on the top of the bird's head (see page 144). Push any remaining yarn tails through the body, and trim.

Who can resist a lovable teddy? Not many people I know!
I hope you will want to find a home for this little cutie
in your Amigurumi collection.

Tiny ted

Finished size

Approx. 1½ x 1½in (3 x 3cm)

Materials

Anchor Pearl Cotton No 8, 100% cotton
 (89yd/81m per 10g ball)
1 x 10g ball of 1025 rose (A)
1.00mm (UK4:US10) crochet hook
Toy stuffing
Large sewing needle
Black embroidery thread
Embroidery needle
2 black seed beads
Beading needle
Approx. 8in (20cm) length of ⅛in (2mm) ribbon

Body

Round 1: Using A, create a slip knot, ch 2.

Round 2: 6 dc into first ch.

Round 3: 2 dc into each dc (12 sts).

Round 4: (1 dc in next dc, dc2inc), rep 6 times (18 sts).

Round 5: (Dc in next 2 dc, dc2inc), rep 6 times (24 sts).

Rounds 6–8: Dc around.

Round 9: (Dc in next 2 dc, dc2tog), rep 6 times (18 sts).

Round 10: Dc around.

Round 11: (1 dc in next dc, dc2tog), rep 6 times (12 sts).

Round 12: Dc around.

Fasten off.

Break yarn, leaving approximately a 6in (15cm) tail.

Head

Round 1: Using A, create a slip knot, ch 2.

Round 2: 6 dc into first ch.

Round 3: 2 dc into each dc (12 sts).

Round 4: (1 dc in next dc, dc2inc), rep 6 times (18 sts).

Rounds 5–7: Dc around.

Round 8: (Dc in next 2 dc, dc2tog) continue to do this until a small hole remains.

Fasten off.

Break yarn, leaving approximately a 6in (15cm) tail.

Legs (make 4)

Round 1: Using A, create a slip knot, ch 2.

Round 2: 6 dc into first ch.

Round 3: (1 dc into next dc, dc2inc), rep 3 times (9 sts).

Rounds 4–6: Dc around.

Fasten off.

Break yarn, leaving approximately a 6in (15cm) tail.

Ears (make 2)

Round 1: Using A, create a slip knot, ch 2.

Round 2: 6 dc into first ch.

Fasten off.

Break yarn, leaving approximately a 6in (15cm) tail.

Making up

Lightly stuff the body, head and legs. Using the yarn tails attached to the separate pieces and mattress stitch (see page 140), stitch the teddy together. Using the embroidery thread and backstitch (see page 140), stitch on the facial details. Stitch on the seed beads for the eyes (see page 142) and tie the ribbon into a bow around the teddy's neck. Trim any excess. Push any remaining yarn tails through the body, and trim.

You don't have to watch the calories with this little treat!
Why not try them out with different coloured toppings? The frosting
is tricky to attach but you will soon get the hang of it.

Cute cupcake

Finished size

Approx. 1 x 1in (2.5 x 2.5cm)

Materials

Anchor Pearl Cotton No 8, 100% cotton
  (89yd/81m per 10g ball)
1 x 10g ball of 26 pink (A)
1 x 10g ball of 301 yellow/cream (B)
1.00mm (UK4:US10) crochet hook
Large sewing needle

Toy stuffing
Red bead
Red sewing or embroidery cotton
Beading needle

Base

Round 1: Using A, create a slip knot, ch 2.

Round 2: 6 dc into first ch.

Round 3: 2 dc into each dc (12 sts).

Round 4: (1 dc in next dc, dc2inc), rep 6 times, place marker (18 sts).

Round 5: (Dc in next 2 dc, dc2inc), rep to marker (24 sts).

Round 6: (Dc in next 3 dc, dc2inc), rep to marker (30 sts).

Rounds 7–8: Dc into back of each dc to marker.

Rounds 9–11: Dc around to marker.

Round 12: (Dc in next 5 dc, dc2inc), rep to marker (35 sts).

Fasten off.

Break yarn, leaving approximately a 6in (15cm) tail.

Top (excluding frosting)

Round 1: Using B, create a slip knot, ch 2.

Round 2: 6 dc into first ch.

Round 3: 2 dc into each dc (12 sts).

Round 4: (1 dc in next dc, dc2inc), rep 6 times, place marker (18 sts).

Round 5: (Dc in next 2 dc, dc2inc), rep to marker (24 sts).

Rounds 6–7: Dc around to marker.

Round 8: (Dc in next 3 dc, dc2inc), rep to marker (30 sts).

Round 9: Dc around to marker.

Round 10: (Dc in next 5 dc, dc2inc), rep to marker (35 sts).

Continue doing this until it fits the top of the base.

Fasten off.

Break yarn, leaving approximately a 6in (15cm) tail.

Frosting

Using B, ch 80.

Row 1: Turn, ch 2, 2 tr into 3rd ch from hook, 1 ch, (3 tr, 1 ch) to end of ch.

This will create a corkscrew effect. Fasten off.

Break yarn, leaving approximately a 6in (15cm) tail.

Making up

Using the yarn tails, stitch the frosting onto the top of the cupcake in a circular motion, starting from the outside and coiling into the centre, then fasten off. Using the yarn tails, stitch the frosted top onto the base using mattress stitch (see page 140), leaving a small gap to place stuffing. When stuffed to the level required, continue to close the gap and fasten off. Stitch on a red bead for a cherry using red sewing cotton. Push any remaining yarn tails through the body, and trim.

Tip

Give your cupcake some extra sprinkle topping by stitching on seed beads (see page 142).

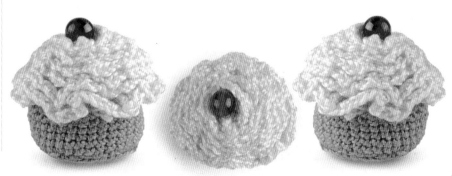

This project could not be easier. The only part that may be difficult is the mane; it might be worth practising before you go on to your final piece. The name was chosen due to the loopy stitches that make up the mane.

Loopy lion

Finished size
Approx. 1 x ¾in (2.5 x 2cm)

Materials
Anchor Pearl Cotton No 8, 100% cotton
  (89yd/81m per 10g ball)
1 x 10g ball of 307 golden brown (A)
1 x 10g ball of 1011 skin colour (B)
1.00mm (UK4:US10) crochet hook
Toy stuffing

Large sewing needle
Black embroidery thread
Dark brown embroidery thread
Embroidery needle

Body

Round 1: Using A, create a slip knot, ch 2.

Round 2: 6 dc into first ch.

Round 3: 2 dc into each dc (12 sts).

Round 4: (1 dc in next dc, dc2inc), rep 6 times (18 sts).

Round 5: (Dc in next 2 dc, dc2inc), rep 6 times (24 sts).

Rounds 6–13: Dc around.

Round 14: (1 dc in next dc, dc2tog), rep 8 times (16 sts).

Round 15: Dc around.

Round 16: (dc in next 2 dc, dc2tog), rep 4 times (12 sts).

Stuff item.

Round 17: Dc2tog around until the hole is closed.

Fasten off.

Break yarn, leaving approximately a 6in (15cm) tail to attach the head. Thread the yarn tail through a large sewing needle. Close any gap left at the top then thread the remainder through the body of the lion, and trim.

Face

Round 1: Using B, create a slip knot, ch 2.

Round 2: 6 dc into first ch.

Round 3: 2 dc into each dc (12 sts).

Round 4: Dc around.

Fasten off.

Break yarn, leaving approximately a 6in (15cm) tail.

Ears (make 2)

Round 1: Using A, create a slip knot, ch 2.

Round 2: 6 dc into first ch.

Fasten off.

Break yarn, leaving approximately a 6in (15cm) tail.

Tail

Row 1: Using A, create a slip knot, ch 10.

Row 2: Turn work, dc into each ch.

Fasten off.

Break yarn, leaving approximately a 6in (15cm) tail.

Making up

Using the yarn tails attached to the separate pieces, stitch the ears and tail into place with mattress stitch (see page 140). Using dark brown embroidery thread, create loops around the face for the mane (see page 143). Using black embroidery thread and backstitch (see page 140), embroider the face details. Using the yarn tails attached to the body and face, stitch the lion together with mattress stitch. Push any remaining yarn tails through the body, and trim.

This pretty little pink piglet should have you squealing with delight. This simple pattern is perfect for crochet beginners and those new to Amigurumi to get to grips with.

Piccolo piglet

Finished size

Approx. ½ x 1in (1.5 x 2.5cm)

Materials

Anchor Pearl Cotton No 8, 100% cotton (89yd/81m per 10g ball)

1 x 10g ball of 52 pink (A)

1.00mm (UK4:US10) crochet hook

Toy stuffing

Large sewing needle

Black embroidery thread

Embroidery needle

2 black seed beads

Beading needle

Body

Round 1: Using A, create a slip knot, ch 2.

Round 2: 6 dc into first ch.

Round 3: 2 dc into each dc (12 sts).

Round 4: (1 dc in next dc, dc2inc), rep 6 times (18 sts).

Rounds 5–12: Dc around.

Round 13: (Dc in next dc, dc2tog), rep 6 times (12 sts).

Round 14: (Dc in next dc, dc2tog), rep 4 times (8 sts).

Stuff item.

Round 15: Dc2tog around until the hole is closed.

Fasten off.

Break yarn, leaving approximately a 6in (15cm) tail.

Thread the yarn tail through a large sewing needle. Close any gap left at the top then thread the remainder through the body of the pig, and trim.

Legs (make 4)

Round 1: Using A, create a slip knot, ch 2.

Round 2: 6 dc into first ch.

Round 3: (Dc in next dc, dc2inc), rep 3 times (9 sts).

Round 4: Dc around.

Fasten off.

Break yarn, leaving approximately a 6in (15cm) tail.

Snout

Round 1: Using A, create a slip knot, ch 2.

Round 2: 6 dc into first ch.

Round 3: Dc into each dc (6 sts).

Fasten off.

Break yarn, leaving approximately a 6in (15cm) tail.

Tail

Row 1: Using A, create a slip knot, ch 7.

Row 2: 2 dc in each ch.

Fasten off.

Break yarn, leaving approximately a 6in (15cm) tail.

Ears (make 2)

Round 1: Using A, create a slip knot, ch 2.

Round 2: 6 dc into first ch.

Fasten off.

Break yarn, leaving approximately a 6in (15cm) tail.

Making up

Lightly stuff the legs. Using the yarn tails attached to the separate pieces, stitch the piglet together with mattress stitch (see page 140). Stitch the legs on first as otherwise you can sometimes make them lopsided. Using black embroidery thread and backstitch (see page 140), embroider the face details. Stitch on the seed beads for the eyes (see page 142). Push any remaining yarn tails through the body, and trim.

Toadstools with red tops and white spots remind me of fairies and magic. Why not create some fairy luck and make this tiny version. It would look great as a pendant or a bracelet charm.

Fairy toadstool

Finished size

Approx. ¾ x ½in (2 x 1.5cm)

Materials

Anchor Pearl Cotton No 8, 100% cotton
   (89yd/81m per 10g ball)
1 x 10g ball of 46 red (A)
1 x 10g ball of 1011 beige (B)
1.00mm (UK4:US10) crochet hook
Toy stuffing
Large sewing needle
Approx. 9 white seed beads
White sewing or embroidery cotton
Beading needle

Top

Round 1: Using A, create a slip knot, ch 2.

Round 2: 6 dc into first ch.

Round 3: 2 dc into each dc (12 sts).

Round 4: 2 dc into each dc (24 sts).

Round 5: Dc around.

Round 6: (Dc in next 2 dc, dc2inc), rep 8 times (32 sts).

Rounds 7–8: Dc around.

Round 9: (Dc in next 2 dc, dc2tog), rep 8 times (24 sts).

Round 10: Dc2tog around until a small hole is left.

Stuff item.

Continue to dc2tog until the hole is closed.

Fasten off.

Break yarn, leaving approximately a 6in (15cm) tail.

Thread the yarn tail through a large sewing needle. Close any gap left at the top then thread the remainder through the body of the top, and trim.

Stem

Round 1: Using B, create a slip knot, ch 2.

Round 2: 6 dc into first ch.

Round 3: 2 dc into each dc (12 sts).

Round 4: (1 dc in next dc, dc2inc), rep 6 times (18 sts).

Rounds 5–6: Dc around.

Round 7: (1 dc in next dc, dc2tog), rep 6 times (12 sts).

Rounds 8–9: Dc around.

Fasten off.

Break yarn, leaving approximately a 6in (15cm) tail.

Making up

Lightly stuff the base. Using the yarn tails attached to the separate pieces, stitch the toadstool together with mattress stitch (see page 140). Using the sewing cotton, stitch the white seed beads to the top (see page 142). Push any remaining yarn tails through the body, and trim.

Tip

If you intend to make this item into a pendant (see page 147) then remember not to stitch beads onto the centre of the top.

They don't come much cooler than this little polar bear.
He has a few more parts to make than my other bears,
and his chubby body is perfect for that cold weather.

Cool dude

Finished size

Approx. 1 x 1in (2.5 x 2.5cm)

Materials

Anchor Pearl Cotton No 8, 100% cotton
    (89yd/81m per 10g ball)
1 x 10g ball of 1 white (A)
1.00mm (UK4:US10) crochet hook
Toy stuffing
Large sewing needle
Black embroidery thread
Embroidery needle
2 black seed beads
Beading needle

Body

Round 1: Using A, create a slip knot, ch 2.

Round 2: 6 dc into first ch.

Round 3: 2 dc into each dc (12 sts).

Round 4: 2 dc into each dc (24 sts).

Round 5: (1 dc in next dc, dc2inc), rep 12 times (36 sts).

Rounds 6–8: Dc around.

Round 9: (Dc in next 4 dc, dc2tog), rep 6 times (30 sts).

Round 10: (Dc in next 3 dc, dc2tog), rep 6 times (24 sts).

Rounds 11–13: Dc around.

Round 14: (Dc in next 2 dc, dc2tog), rep 6 times (18 sts).

Round 15: (1 dc in next dc, dc2tog), rep 6 times (12 sts).

Round 16: (1 dc in next dc, dc2tog), rep 4 times (8 sts).

Fasten off.

Break yarn, leaving approximately a 6in (15cm) tail.

Muzzle

Round 1: Using A, create a slip knot, ch 2.

Round 2: 6 dc into first ch.

Round 3: (1 dc in next dc, dc2inc), rep 3 times (9 sts).

Fasten off.

Break yarn, leaving approximately a 6in (15cm) tail.

Tail

Round 1: Using A, create a slip knot, ch 2.

Round 2: 6 dc into first ch.

Round 3: (1 dc in next dc, dc2inc), rep 3 times (9 sts).

Fasten off.

Break yarn, leaving approximately a 6in (15cm) tail.

Legs (make 4)

Round 1: Using A, create a slip knot, ch 2.

Round 2: 6 dc into first ch.

Round 3: (1 dc in next dc, dc2inc), rep 3 times (9 sts).

Round 4: Dc around.

Fasten off.

Break yarn, leaving approximately a 6in (15cm) tail.

Ears (make 2)

Round 1: Using A, create a slip knot, ch 2.

Round 2: 6 dc into first ch.

Fasten off.

Break yarn, leaving approximately a 6in (15cm) tail.

Making up

Lightly stuff the body and legs. Using the yarn tails attached to the separate pieces, stitch the ears, nose and tail into place with mattress stitch (see page 140), then stitch the polar bear together. Using the embroidery thread and backstitch (see page 140), embroider the face details. Stitch on the seed beads for the eyes (see page 142). Push any remaining yarn tails through the body, and trim.

This simple project is a great one for beginners to start off with. My children's passion for pink frosted doughnuts with sprinkles was the inspiration behind this little confectionery item.

Frosted doughnut

Finished size

Approx. ¼ x ¾in (1 x 2cm)

Materials

Anchor Pearl Cotton No 8, 100% cotton
  (89yd/81m per 10g ball)
1 x 10g ball of 933 beige (A)
1 x 10g ball of 26 pink (B)
1.00mm (UK4:US10) crochet hook

Toy stuffing
Large sewing needle
Approx. 15–20 assorted colours of seed beads
Pink sewing or embroidery cotton
Beading needle

Base

Round 1: Using A, create a slip knot, ch 2.

Round 2: 6 dc into first ch.

Round 3: 2 dc into each dc (12 sts).

Round 4: 2 dc into each dc, place marker (24 sts).

Round 5: (Dc in next 2 dc, dc2inc), rep around to marker (32 sts).

Rounds 6–8: Dc around to marker.

Round 9: (Dc in next 2 dc, dc2tog), rep to marker (24 sts).

Round 10: (1 dc in next dc, dc2tog), rep to marker (16 sts).

Round 11: Dc2tog until a small hole is left.

Stuff item.

Continue to dc2tog until the hole is closed.

Fasten off.

Break yarn, leaving approximately a 6in (15cm) tail.

Thread the yarn tail through a large sewing needle. Close any gap left at the top then thread the remainder through the base, and trim.

Frosting

Round 1: Using B, create a slip knot, ch 2.

Round 2: 6 dc into first ch.

Round 3: 2 dc into each dc (12 sts).

Round 4: 2 dc into each dc, place marker (24 sts).

Round 5: (Dc in next 2 dc, dc2inc), rep around to marker (32 sts).

Round 6: (3 tr in next dc, dc in next 2 dc), rep to marker.

Fasten off.

Break yarn, leaving approximately a 6in (15cm) tail.

Making up

Using the sewing cotton, stitch the seed beads onto the frosting to create the sprinkle covering (see page 142). Using the yarn tail attached to the frosting, stitch the frosting to the base with mattress stitch (see page 140), following the edge. Push any remaining yarn tails through the body, and trim.

Tip

These doughnuts would make a lovely garland for a necklace, especially with many different colours of frosting on top.

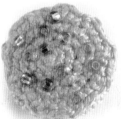

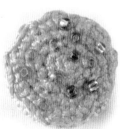

I couldn't have a book about Amigurumi without the beautiful Japanese Kokeshi doll, which first inspired me to try this rewarding style of crochet.

Kokeshi doll

Finished size

Approx. 1½ x ¾in (3.5 x 2cm)

Materials

Anchor Pearl Cotton No 8, 100% cotton
   (89yd/81m per 10g ball)
1 x 10g ball of 46 red or 228 green (A)
1 x 10g ball of 403 black (B)
1 x 10g ball of 1011 skin colour (C)
1.00mm (UK4:US10) crochet hook
Toy stuffing

Large sewing needle
Black embroidery thread
Red embroidery thread
Embroidery needle
Pink flower sequin
Pink seed bead
Pink embroidery thread
Beading needle

Body

Round 1: Using A, create a slip knot, ch 2.

Round 2: 6 dc into first ch.

Round 3: 2 dc into each st (12 sts).

Round 4: (1 dc in next dc, dc2inc), rep 6 times, place marker (18 sts).

Round 5: Dc around to marker.

Round 6: (Dc in next 2 dc, dc2inc), rep around to marker (24 sts).

Rounds 7–11: Dc around to marker.

Round 12: (Dc in next 2 dc, dc2tog), rep to marker (18 sts).

Round 13: Dc around to marker.

Round 14: (1 dc in next dc, dc2tog), rep to marker (12 sts).

Rounds 15–16: Dc around to marker. Stuff item.

Round 17: Dc2tog around until only a small hole is left.

Fasten off.

Break yarn, leaving approximately a 6in (15cm) tail.

Head

Round 1: Using B, create a slip knot, ch 2.

Round 2: 6 dc into first ch.

Round 3: 2 dc into each st, place marker (12 sts).

Round 4: (1 dc in next dc, dc2inc), rep 6 times (18 sts).

Rounds 5–6: Dc around to marker.

Round 7: (Dc in next 2 dc, dc2inc), rep to marker (24 sts).

Change to C.

Rounds 8–9: Dc around to marker.

Round 10: (Dc in next 2 dc, dc2tog), rep to marker (18 sts).

Stuff item.

Round 11: Dc2tog around until only a small hole is left.

Fasten off.

Break yarn, leaving approximately a 6in (15cm) tail.

Hair buns (make 2)

Round 1: Using B, create a slip knot, ch 2.

Round 2: 6 dc into first ch.

Round 3: 2 dc into each st (12 sts).

Fasten off.

Break yarn, leaving approximately a 6in (15cm) tail.

Making up

Using the yarn tails attached to the separate pieces, stitch the doll together with mattress stitch (see page 140). Using the black and red embroidery threads and backstitch (see page 140), embroider the face and dress details. Using the pink embroidery thread, stitch the seed bead with the sequin to the doll's head. Push any remaining yarn tails through the body, and trim.

Don't worry, there's no painful sting in this little lady
– she only concerns herself with honey and flowers
and really is as sweet as can bee!

Honey bee

Finished size
Approx. ¾ x 1½in (2 x 3cm)

Materials
Anchor Pearl Cotton No 8, 100% cotton
   (89yd/81m per 10g ball)
1 x 10g ball of 403 black (A)
1 x 10g ball of 295 yellow (B)
1 x 10g ball of 1 white (C)
1.00mm (UK4:US10) crochet hook

Toy stuffing
Large sewing needle
2 black seed beads
Black sewing or embroidery cotton
Beading needle

Body

Round 1: Using A, create a slip knot, ch 2.

Round 2: 6 dc into first ch.

Round 3: Dc in each dc.

Round 4: 2 dc into each dc (12 sts).

Round 5: Dc in each dc.

Change to B.

Round 6: Dc in each dc.

Round 7: 2 dc into each dc. Use colour changeover as your marker (24 sts).

Round 8: Dc in each dc.

Change to A.

Rounds 9–11: Dc around to marker.

Change to B.

Rounds 12–14: Dc around to marker.

Change to A.

Round 15: Dc2tog to marker (12 sts). Stuff item.

Round 16: Dc2tog around until the hole is closed.

Fasten off.

Break yarn, leaving approximately a 6in (15cm) tail.

Thread the yarn tail through a large sewing needle. Close any gap left at the top then thread the remainder through the body of the bee, and trim.

Wings (make 2)

Round 1: Using C, create a slip knot, ch 2.

Round 2: 6 dc into first ch.

Round 3: 2 dc into each dc (12sts).

Fasten off.

Break yarn, leaving approximately a 6in (15cm) tail.

Making up

Using the yarn tails attached to the wings, stitch into place with mattress stitch (see page 140). Using long lengths of shade A, thread through and fasten to the body for legs (see page 145). Stitch the seed beads on for the eyes (see page 142). Push any spare thread through the body, and trim.

Tip

When creating stripes, it is a good idea to tie together the threads when you change colours at the ends of rows.

This furry friend is a much-loved pet for many families. If you are unable to house a real version of this adorable animal then perhaps you could find a spot for this miniature version instead.

Funny bunny

Finished size
Approx. ½ x 1½in (1.5 x 3cm)

Materials
Anchor Pearl Cotton No 8, 100% cotton
   (89yd/81m per 10g ball)
1 x 10g ball of 129 blue (A)
1 x 10g ball of 1 white (B)
1.00mm (UK4:US10) crochet hook
Toy stuffing

Large sewing needle
Black embroidery thread
Embroidery needle
2 black seed beads
Beading needle

Body

Round 1: Using A, create a slip knot, ch 2.

Round 2: 6 dc into first ch.

Round 3: 2 dc into each dc (12 sts).

Round 4: (1 dc in next dc, dc2inc), rep 6 times, place marker (18 sts).

Rounds 5–14: Dc around to marker.

Round 15: (1 dc in next dc, dc2tog), rep to marker (12 sts).

Round 16: (1 dc in next dc, dc2tog), rep to marker (8 sts).

Stuff item.

Round 17: Dc2tog around until the hole is closed.

Fasten off.

Break yarn, leaving approximately a 6in (15cm) tail.

Thread the yarn tail through a large sewing needle. Close any gap left at the top then thread the remainder through the body of the bunny, and trim.

Legs (make 4)

Round 1: Using A, create a slip knot, ch 2.

Round 2: 6 dc into first ch.

Round 3: 1 dc into each dc (6 sts).

Fasten off.

Break yarn, leaving approximately a 6in (15cm) tail.

Tail

As for legs, using B.

Ears (make 2)

Round 1: Using A, create a slip knot, ch 2.

Round 2: 6 dc into first ch.

Round 3: 1 dc into each dc (6 sts).

Continue working these 6 sts until ears are the required length.

Fasten off.

Break yarn, leaving approximately a 6in (15cm) tail.

Use the end of the hook to carefully push the item into shape, right side out.

Making up

Using the yarn tails attached to the separate pieces, stitch the ears and tail into place, then stitch the bunny together with mattress stitch (see page 140). Using the embroidery thread and backstitch (see page 140), embroider the nose and whiskers. Stitch on the seed beads for the eyes (see pages 142). Push any remaining yarn tails through the body, and trim.

A pair of these fortune cookies would make great earrings and hopefully contain a message of good health and luck. The pattern format is a little different from the others but it is simple to make.

Fortune cookie

Finished size

Approx. 1 x 1in (2.5 x 2.5cm)

Materials

Anchor Pearl Cotton No 8, 100% cotton
   (89yd/81m per 10g ball)
1 x 10g ball of 301 cream (A)
1.00mm (UK4:US10) crochet hook
Large sewing needle
Toy stuffing
8 brown and purple seed beads
Light brown embroidery thread
Beading needle

Cookie

Round 1: Using A, create a slip knot, ch 2.

Round 2: 10 dc into first ch.

Round 3: 2 dc into each dc (20 sts).

Round 4: (1 dc in next dc, dc2inc), rep 10 times (30 sts).

Round 5: (1 dc in next 2 dc, dc2inc), rep 10 times (40 sts).

Round 6: (1 dc in next 3 dc, dc2inc), rep 10 times (50 sts).

Round 7: (1 dc in next dc, dc2inc), rep 25 times (75 sts).

Round 8: Dc around.

Fasten off.

Break yarn, leaving approximately a 6in (15cm) tail.

Making up

Fold the cookie in half and stitch together using the yarn tail and mattress stitch (see page 140), leaving a small gap. Stuff, then continue to stitch up. Using the embroidery thread, stitch the seed beads along the edge (see page 142).

Tip

Why not tone the colours in with your favourite outfit by changing the colour of the seed beads around the edge?

It's hard to resist a puppy. Although I have created these cuties in the colours stated, you could really indulge yourself and make as many colour combinations as you wish to create a complete puppy world.

Puppy love

Finished size
Approx. 1 x ¾in (2.5 x 2cm)

Materials
Anchor Pearl Cotton No 8, 100% cotton
   (89yd/81m per 10g ball)
1 x 10g ball of 907 golden brown (A)
Small amount of 358 chocolate brown (B)
1.00mm (UK4:US10) crochet hook
Toy stuffing
Large sewing needle

Black embroidery thread
Golden brown embroidery thread to stitch on chain
Embroidery needle
Approx. 1½in (4cm) fine chain (measure around
   puppy's neck before cutting to size)

Body

Round 1: Using A, create a slip knot, ch 2.

Round 2: 6 dc into first ch.

Round 3: 2 dc into each st (12 sts).

Round 4: 2 dc into each st (24 sts).

Round 5: (1 dc in next dc, dc2inc), rep around, place marker (36 sts).

Rounds 6–9: Dc around.

Round 10: (Dc in next 2 dc, dc2tog), rep to marker (27 sts).

Round 11: (1 dc in next dc, dc2tog), rep to marker (18 sts).

Rounds 12–15: Dc around to marker.

Round 16: (1 dc in next dc, dc2tog) to marker (12 sts).

Round 17: Dc around to marker. Stuff item.

Round 18: Dc2tog around until the hole is closed.

Fasten off.

Break yarn, leaving approximately a 6in (15cm) tail.

Thread the yarn tail through a large sewing needle. Close any gap left at the top then thread the remainder through the body of the puppy, and trim.

Ears (make 2)

Round 1: Using B, create a slip knot, ch 2.

Round 2: 6 dc into first ch.

Round 3: 2 dc into each st (12 sts).

Fasten off.

Break yarn leaving approximately a 6in (15cm) tail.

Tail

Row 1: Using B, create a slip knot, ch 16.

Row 2: Turn work, dc into each ch.

Fasten off.

Break yarn, leaving approximately a 6in (15cm) tail.

Making up

Using the yarn tails attached to the separate pieces, stitch the ears and tail into place with mattress stitch (see page 140). Using the black embroidery thread and backstitch (see page 140), embroider the face details. Using the golden brown embroidery thread, stitch the chain to the puppy's neck to make a collar. Push any remaining yarn tails through the body, and trim.

> *Tip*
> *You could add a bead or two or a tiny charm onto the collar as a name tag.*

This little turtle is an easy design. For the embroidered top, you could indulge your creativity and perhaps put on someone's initials or design a flower.

Tom turtle

Finished size
Approx. ¼ x 1⅜in (1 x 3.5cm)

Materials
Anchor Pearl Cotton No 8, 100% cotton
  (89yd/81m per 10g ball)
1 x 10g ball of 213 green (A)
1 x 10g ball of 378 mink (B)
1.00mm (UK4:US10) crochet hook
Brown embroidery thread

Embroidery needle
Toy stuffing
Large sewing needle
2 black seed beads
Black sewing or embroidery cotton
Beading needle

Top of shell

Round 1: Using A, create a slip knot, ch 2.

Round 2: 6 dc into first ch.

Round 3: 2 dc into each dc (12 sts).

Round 4: Dc around.

Round 5: (1 dc in next dc, dc2inc), rep 6 times (18 sts).

Round 6: Dc around.

Round 7: (Dc in next 2 dc, dc2inc), rep 6 times (24 sts).

Round 8: (Dc in next 2 dc, dc2inc), rep 8 times (32 sts).

Change to B.

Round 9: (1 dc, 1 tr), rep 16 times. Join with ss at base of first dc.

Fasten off.

Break yarn, leaving approximately a 6in (15cm) tail.

Under-shell

Round 1: Using A, create a slip knot, ch 2.

Round 2: 6 dc into first ch.

Round 3: 2 dc into each dc (12 sts).

Round 4: Dc around.

Round 5: (1 dc in next dc, dc2inc), rep 6 times (18 sts).

Round 6: Dc around.

Round 7: (Dc in next 2 dc, dc2inc), rep 6 times (24 sts).

Round 8: (Dc in next 2 dc, dc2inc), rep 8 times (32 sts).

Fasten off.

Break yarn, leaving approximately a 6in (15cm) tail.

Head

Round 1: Using A, create a slip knot, ch 2.

Round 2: 6 dc into first ch.

Round 3: 2 dc into each dc (12 sts).

Rounds 4–6: Dc around.

Fasten off.

Break yarn, leaving approximately a 6in (15cm) tail.

Legs (make 4)

Round 1: Using A, create a slip knot, ch 2.

Round 2: 6 dc into first ch.

Rounds 3–4: Dc around.

Fasten off.

Break yarn, leaving approximately a 6in (15cm) tail.

Making up

Using brown embroidery thread and backstitch (see page 140), stitch on the shell design, then stitch the shell top to the base of the body. Lightly stuff all the body parts. Using the yarn tails attached to the separate pieces, stitch the turtle together with mattress stitch (see page 140). Using the sewing cotton, stitch on the seed beads for the eyes (see page 142).

This angelic little lady can go wherever you travel, perhaps on a bag charm or keyring. She would make a marvellous gift for a best friend or special family member.

Angel delight

Finished size

Approx. 1⅜ x 1in (3.5 x 2.5cm)

Materials

Anchor Pearl Cotton No 8, 100% cotton
   (89yd/81m per 10g ball)
1 x 10g ball of 1 white (A)
1 x 10g ball of 305 yellow (B)
1 x 10g ball of 1011 skin colour (C)
1.00mm (UK4:US10) crochet hook
Toy stuffing
Large sewing needle

Blue embroidery thread
Pink embroidery thread
Embroidery needle
Approx. 16 gold seed beads (measure around
   bun to decide on final number)
Gold or yellow sewing or embroidery cotton
Beading needle

Body

Round 1: Using A, create a slip knot, ch 2.

Round 2: 6 dc into first ch.

Round 3: 2 dc into each dc (12 sts).

Round 4: (1 dc in next dc, dc2inc), rep 6 times (18 sts).

Round 5: (Dc in next 2 dc, dc2inc), rep 6 times (24 sts).

Round 6: (Dc in next 2 dc, dc2inc), rep 8 times (32 sts).

Rounds 7–8: Dc around.

Round 9: (Dc in next 2 dc, dc2tog), rep 8 times (24 sts).

Round 10: (Dc in next 2 dc, dc2tog), rep 6 times (18 sts).

Rounds 11–12: Dc around.

Round 13: (1 dc in next dc, dc2tog), rep 6 times (12 sts).

Fasten off.

Break yarn, leaving approximately a 6in (15cm) tail.

Stuff item.

Thread the yarn tail through a large sewing needle. Close any gap left at the top then thread the remainder through the body of the doll, and trim.

Head

Round 1: Using B, create a slip knot, ch 2.

Round 2: 6 dc into first ch.

Round 3: 2 dc into each dc (12 sts).

Round 4: (1 dc in next dc, dc2inc), rep 6 times (18 sts).

Rounds 5–8: Dc around.

Change to C.

Rounds 9–11: Dc around.

Round 12: (1 dc in next dc, dc2tog), rep 6 times (12 sts).

Round 13: (1 dc in next dc, dc2tog), rep 4 times (8 sts).

Fasten off.

Break yarn, leaving approximately a 6in (15cm) tail.

Stuff item.

Wings (make 2)

Round 1: Using A, create a slip knot, ch 2.

Round 2: 6 dc into first ch.

Round 3: 2 dc into each dc (12 sts).

Round 4: 2 dc into each dc (24 sts).

Round 5: Dc around.

Fasten off.

Break yarn, leaving approximately a 6in (15cm) tail.

Hair bun

Round 1: Using B, create a slip knot, ch 2.

Round 2: 6 dc into first ch.

Round 3: 2 dc into each dc (12 sts).

Rounds 4–5: Dc around.

Fasten off.

Break yarn, leaving approximately a 6in (15cm) tail.

Making up

Using the yarn tails attached to the separate pieces, stitch the angel together with mattress stitch (see page 140). Using blue embroidery thread, embroider the eyes, and using the pink thread, embroider the mouth and dress details with backstitch (see page 140). Using the gold or yellow cotton, make a string of seed beads and stitch on to create a crown or halo (see page 142).

Pandas are such popular animals that this one will be in great demand. This round little fellow is easy to make, but be careful to fasten your ends off when changing colours.

Panda-monium

Finished size
Approx. 1¼ x 1¼in (3 x 3cm)

Materials
Anchor Pearl Cotton No 8, 100% cotton
   (89yd/81m per 10g ball)
1 x 10g ball of 1 white (A)
1 x 10g ball of 403 black (B)
1.00mm (UK4:US10) crochet hook

Toy stuffing
Large sewing needle
2 black seed beads
Beading needle
Black embroidery thread
Embroidery needle

Body

Round 1: Using A, create a slip knot, ch 2.

Round 2: 6 dc into first ch.

Round 3: 2 dc into each dc (12 sts).

Round 4: 2 dc into each dc, place marker (24 sts).

Rounds 5–8: Dc around to marker. Change to B.

Rounds 9–11: Dc around to marker. Change to A.

Rounds 12–14: Dc around to marker.

Round 15: (1 dc in next dc, dc2tog), rep to marker (16 sts).

Round 16: (Dc in next 2 dc, dc2tog), rep to marker (12 sts).
Stuff item.

Round 17: Dc2tog around until the hole is closed.
Fasten off.

Break yarn, leaving approximately a 6in (15cm) tail.

Thread the yarn tail through a large sewing needle. Close any gap left at the top then thread the remainder through the body, and trim.

Eye rims (make 2)

Round 1: Using B, create a slip knot, ch 2.

Round 2: 7 dc into first ch.
Fasten off.

Break yarn, leaving approximately a 6in (15cm) tail.

Legs (make 4)

Round 1: Using B, create a slip knot, ch 2.

Round 2: 6 dc into first ch.

Round 3: 2 dc into each dc, place marker (12 sts).

Rounds 4–5: Dc around to marker.
Fasten off.

Break yarn, leaving approximately a 6in (15cm) tail.

Using the end of the crochet hook, carefully push leg into shape, turning right side out.

Ears (make 2)

Round 1: Using B, create a slip knot, ch 2.

Round 2: 6 dc into first ch.
Fasten off.

Break yarn, leaving approximately a 6in (15cm) tail.

Making up

Lightly stuff the legs. Using the yarn tails attached to the separate pieces, stitch on the legs and ears with mattress stitch (see page 140). Using the yarn tails, stitch on the eye rims then stitch the seed bead to the centre (see page 142). Using the black embroidery thread and backstitch (see page 140), embroider a nose and mouth. Push any remaining yarn tails through the body, and trim.

What a pretty sight it is to see a butterfly on a summer day. Although I have chosen these particular colours, you can pick your own shades to match your favourite outfits.

Flutterby butterfly

Finished size

Approx. 1¼ x 1⅜in (3 x 3.5cm)

Materials

Anchor Pearl Cotton No 8, 100% cotton
   (89yd/81m per 10g ball)
1 x 10g ball of 403 black (A)
1 x 10g ball of 110 purple (B)
1 x 10g ball of 128 pale blue (C)
1 x 10g ball of 433 dark blue (D)
1.00mm (UK4:US10) crochet hook

Toy stuffing
Large sewing needle
2 blue seed beads
2 purple seed beads
Purple sewing or embroidery cotton
Beading needle

Body

Round 1: Using A, create a slip knot, ch 2.

Round 2: 6 dc into first ch.

Round 3: Dc in each dc (6 sts).

Round 4: (1 dc in next dc, dc2inc), place marker (9 sts).

Rounds 5–7: Dc around to marker.

Round 8: (Dc in next 2 dc, dc2inc), rep to marker (12 sts).

Rounds 9–14: Dc around to marker. Stuff item.

Round 15: Dc2tog around until the hole is closed.

Fasten off.

Break yarn, leaving approximately a 6in (15cm) tail.

Thread the yarn tail through a large sewing needle. Close any gap left at the top then thread the remainder through the body of the butterfly, and trim.

Large wings (make 2)

Round 1: Using B, create a slip knot, ch 2.

Round 2: 6 dc into first ch.

Round 3: 2 dc into each dc (12 sts). Change to C.

Round 4: 2 dc into each dc (24 sts). Change to D.

Round 5: Dc into each dc.

Fasten off.

Break yarn, leaving approximately a 6in (15cm) tail.

Small wings (make 2)

Round 1: Using C, create a slip knot, ch 2.

Round 2: 6 dc into first ch.

Round 3: 2 dc into each dc (12 sts). Change to B.

Round 4: 2 dc into each dc.

Fasten off.

Break yarn, leaving approximately a 6in (15cm) tail.

Wing tips

Row 5: Using D, ss into any stitch, dc into next 3 dc, turn.

Row 6: Ch 1, dc in 2nd and 3rd dc, turn.

Row 7: Ch 1, dc2tog.

Fasten off.

Break yarn, leaving approximately a 6in (15cm) tail.

Making up

Using the yarn tails attached to the wings, stitch to the body with mattress stitch (see page 140). Using a short length of yarn in shade A, push through the head end of the body to make antennae (see page 145). Stitch on the purple seed beads for the eyes (see page 142) and the blue seed beads to embellish the wings. Push any remaining yarn tails through the body, and trim.

This funny and endearing bird is always a firm favourite.
Why not make him as a companion to the polar bear
(see page 34) so they can play fun games together?

Polar penguin

Finished size

Approx. 1 x 1in (2.5 x 2.5cm)

Materials

Anchor Pearl Cotton No 8, 100% cotton
   (89yd/81m per 10g ball)
1 x 10g ball of 403 black (A)
1 x 10g ball of 1 white (B)
1 x 10g ball of 303 orange (C)
1.00mm (UK4:US10) crochet hook
Toy stuffing
Large sewing needle
Blue embroidery thread
Embroidery needle

Body

Round 1: Using A, create a slip knot, ch 2.

Round 2: 6 dc into first ch.

Round 3: 2 dc into each dc (12 sts).

Round 4: 2 dc into each dc, place marker (24 sts).

Round 5: (Dc in next 2 dc, dc2inc), rep around to marker (32 sts).

Rounds 6–12: Dc around to marker.

Round 13: (Dc in next 2 dc, dc2tog), rep to marker (24 sts).

Round 14: (1 dc in next dc, dc2tog), rep to marker (16 sts).

Round 15: Dc around to marker. Stuff item.

Round 16: Dc2tog around until the hole is closed.

Fasten off.

Break yarn, leaving approximately a 6in (15cm) tail.

Thread the yarn tail through a large sewing needle. Close any gap left at the top then thread the remainder through the body of the penguin, and trim.

Chest

Round 1: Using B, create a slip knot, ch 2.

Round 2: 6 dc into first ch.

Round 3: 2 dc into each dc (12 sts).

Round 4: 2 dc into each dc (24 sts). Fasten off.

Break yarn, leaving approximately a 6in (15cm) tail.

Wings (make 2)

Round 1: Using A, create a slip knot, ch 2.

Round 2: 6 dc into first ch.

Round 3: 2 dc into each dc (12 sts). Fasten off.

Break yarn, leaving approximately a 6in (15cm) tail.

Feet (make 2)

Round 1: Using C, create a slip knot, ch 2.

Round 2: 6 dc into first ch. Fasten off.

Break yarn, leaving approximately a 6in (15cm) tail.

Making up

Using the yarn tails attached to the separate pieces, stitch the chest, wings and feet into place with mattress stitch (see page 140). Embroider the beak using shade C, by making two French knots on top of each other so they stick out (see page 141). Using the blue embroidery thread and backstitch (see page 140), embroider on the eyes. Push any remaining yarn tails through the body, and trim.

I love the snow, so this little fellow always makes me smile. He is easy to make, but be careful to keep your hands nice and clean when working with white yarn.

Super snowman

Finished size

Approx. 1⅜ x ½in (3.5 x 1.5cm)

Materials

Anchor Pearl Cotton No 8, 100% cotton
   (89yd/81m per 10g ball)
1 x 10g ball of 1 white (A)
1 x 10g ball of 46 red (B)
1.00mm (UK4:US10) crochet hook
Toy stuffing

Large sewing needle
Orange embroidery cotton
Embroidery needle
5 black seed beads
Black embroidery thread
Beading needle

Body

Round 1: Using A, create a slip knot, ch 2.

Round 2: 6 dc into first ch.

Round 3: 2 dc into each dc (12 sts).

Round 4: (1 dc in next dc, dc2inc), rep 6 times, place marker (18 sts).

Round 5: Dc around to marker.

Round 6: (Dc in next 2 dc, dc2inc), rep around to marker (24 sts).

Rounds 7–10: Dc around to marker.

Round 11: (Dc in next 2 dc, dc2tog), rep to marker (18 sts).

Round 12: Dc around to marker.

Round 13: (1 dc in next dc, dc2tog), rep to marker (12 sts).

Round 14: (Dc in next 2 dc, dc2tog), rep to marker (9 sts).

Stuff item.

Round 15: Dc2tog around until a small hole is left.

Fasten off.

Break yarn, leaving approximately a 6in (15cm) tail.

Head

Round 1: Using A, create a slip knot, ch 2.

Round 2: 6 dc into first ch.

Round 3: 2 dc into each dc, place marker (12 sts).

Round 4: (1 dc in next dc, dc2inc), rep 6 times (18 sts).

Rounds 5–8: Dc around to marker.

Round 9: (1 dc in next dc, dc2tog), rep to marker (12 sts).

Round 10: (1 dc in next dc, dc2tog), rep to marker (8 sts).

Fasten off.

Break yarn, leaving approximately a 6in (15cm) tail.

Stuff item.

Hat

Round 1: Using B, create a slip knot, ch 2.

Round 2: 6 dc into first ch.

Round 3: 2 dc into each dc, place marker (12 sts).

Rounds 4–7: Dc around to marker. Allow last row to curl up for hat edge.

Fasten off.

Break yarn, leaving approximately a 6in (15cm) tail.

Scarf

Using B, ch 25.

Row 1: Turn, ch 1 then dc into 2nd ch, dc to the end.

Fasten off.

Thread remaining yarn through scarf, and trim.

Making up

Using the yarn tails attached to the separate pieces, stitch the snowman together with mattress stitch (see page 140). Using the orange thread, make three French knots, one on top of the other, for his nose (see page 141). Using the black embroidery thread, stitch on two seed beads for his eyes and three for his buttons (see page 142). Using the yarn tails and a short length of shade B, stitch the hat and scarf on to complete. Push any remaining tails through the body, and trim.

A perfect project to make as a special gift for all horse- and animal-lovers. I don't think this little one will win any races but she is gorgeous all the same.

Pony pal

Finished size

Approx. 1¼ × 1¼ in (3 × 3cm)

Materials

Anchor Pearl Cotton No 8, 100% cotton
   (89yd/81m per 10g ball)
1 × 10g ball of 378 mink (A)
1.00mm (UK4:US10) crochet hook
Toy stuffing
Large sewing needle
Black embroidery thread
Embroidery needle
2 black seed beads
Beading needle
Approx. 8in (20cm) length of ⅛in (2mm) red ribbon

Body

Round 1: Using A, create a slip knot, ch 2.

Round 2: 6 dc into first ch.

Round 3: 2 dc into each dc (12 sts).

Round 4: (1 dc in next dc, dc2inc), rep 6 times (18 sts).

Rounds 5–11: Dc around.

Round 12: (1 dc in next dc, dc2tog), rep 6 times (12 sts).

Round 13: Dc around.

Stuff item.

Round 14: Dc2tog around until the hole is closed.

Fasten off.

Break yarn, leaving approximately a 6in (15cm) tail.

Thread the yarn tail through a large sewing needle. Close any gap left at the top then thread the remainder through the body, and trim.

Head

Round 1: Using A, create a slip knot, ch 2.

Round 2: 6 dc into first ch.

Round 3: 2 dc into each dc (12 sts).

Round 4: (1 dc in next dc, dc2inc), rep 6 times (18 sts).

Rounds 5–7: Dc around.

Round 8: (1 dc in next dc, dc2tog), rep 6 times (12 sts).

Stuff item.

Round 9: Dc2tog around until the hole is closed.

Fasten off.

Break yarn, leaving approximately a 6in (15cm) tail.

Thread the yarn tail through a large sewing needle. Close any gap left at the top then thread the remainder through the body, and trim.

Legs (make 4)

Round 1: Using A, create a slip knot, ch 2.

Round 2: 6 dc into first ch.

Round 3: (1 dc in next dc, dc2inc), rep 3 times (9 sts).

Rounds 4–5: Dc around.

Fasten off.

Break yarn, leaving approximately a 6in (15cm) tail.

Ears (make 2)

Round 1: Using A, create a slip knot, ch 2.

Round 2: 6 dc into first ch.

Round 3: Dc in next 2 dc.

Fasten off.

Break yarn, leaving approximately a 6in (15cm) tail.

Making up

Lightly stuff the legs. Using the yarn tails attached to the separate pieces, stitch the pony together with mattress stitch (see page 140). For the tail, make a long tuft from the embroidery thread about ½in (1.5cm) long (see page 144). Then make multiple tufts on the head and neck to form the mane and trim as necessary. Using the embroidery thread and backstitch (see page 140), embroider the mouth. Stitch on the seed beads for the eyes (see page 142). Push any remaining yarn tails through the body, and trim. Tie the ribbon into a bow around the pony's neck. Trim any excess.

These juicy-looking strawberries are almost good enough
to eat and remind me of a perfect midsummer's day.
Make them in batches for added impact.

Strawberry sensation

Finished size

Approx. ¾ × ½in (2 × 1.5cm)

Materials

Anchor Pearl Cotton No 8, 100% cotton
   (89yd/81m per 10g ball)
1 × 10g ball of 46 red (A)
1 × 10g ball of 228 green (B)
1.00mm (UK4:US10) crochet hook
Toy stuffing
Large sewing needle
Embroidery needle

Main fruit

Round 1: Using A, create a slip knot, ch 2.

Round 2: 6 dc into first ch.

Round 3: 2 dc into each st (12 sts).

Rounds 4–5: Dc around.

Round 6: (1 dc in next dc, dc2inc), rep around, place marker (18 sts).

Rounds 7–8: Dc around.

Round 9: (1 dc in next dc, dc2tog), rep to marker (12 sts).

Round 10: (1 dc in next dc, dc2tog), rep to marker (8 sts).

Stuff item.

Round 11: Dc2tog around until the hole is closed.

Fasten off.

Break yarn, leaving approximately a 6in (15cm) tail.

Thread the yarn tail through a large sewing needle. Close any gap left at the top then thread the remainder through the body of the strawberry, and trim.

Tip

Once you have finished making your strawberries, roll them around in your palm to plump them up and create a nice shape. Make sure you have clean hands though!

Leaf (make 2 or more)

Round 1: Using B, create a slip knot, ch 2.

Round 2: 6 dc into first ch.

Fasten off.

Break yarn, leaving approximately a 6in (15cm) tail.

Making up

Using the yarn tail attached to the leaves, stitch into place. Embroider pips on to the fruit using shade B. Push any remaining tails through the fruit, and trim.

This little frog is an easy project as it uses just one colour, but it does have lots of parts to sew up. Take your time and don't be daunted – he will be worth the effort.

Hoppy frog

Finished size

Approx. 1 x 1in (2.5 x 2.5cm)

Materials

Anchor Pearl Cotton No 8, 100% cotton
  (89yd/81m per 10g ball)
1 x 10g of 259 green (A)
1.00mm (UK4:US10) crochet hook
Toy stuffing
Large sewing needle
Black embroidery thread
Embroidery needle
2 black seed beads
Beading needle

Body

Round 1: Using A, create a slip knot, ch 2.

Round 2: 6 dc into first ch.

Round 3: 2 dc into each dc, place marker (12 sts).

Round 4: (Dc in next 2 dc, dc2inc), rep around to marker (16 sts).

Round 5: (Dc in next 3 dc, dc2inc), rep around to marker (20 sts).

Round 6: (Dc in next 4 dc, dc2inc), rep around to marker (24 sts).

Round 7: (Dc in next 5 dc, dc2inc), rep around to marker (28 sts).

Rounds 8–10: Dc around to marker.

Round 11: (Dc in next 5 dc, dc2tog), rep to marker (24 sts).

Round 12: Dc around to marker.

Round 13: (Dc in next 4 dc, dc2tog), rep to marker (20 sts).

Round 14: (Dc in next 3 dc, dc2tog), rep to marker (16 sts).

Round 15: (Dc in next 2 dc, dc2tog), rep to marker (12 sts).

Round 16: (1 dc in next dc, dc2tog), rep to marker (8 sts).

Stuff item.

Round 17: Dc2tog around until the hole is closed.

Fasten off. Break yarn, leaving approximately a 6in (15cm) tail.

Thread the yarn tail through a large sewing needle. Close any gap left at the top then thread the remainder through the body of the frog, and trim.

Eyes (make 2)

Round 1: Using A, create a slip knot, ch 2.

Round 2: 6 dc into first ch.

Round 3: 2 dc into each dc (12 sts). Using the end of the crochet hook carefully push into a small dome shape, right side out.

Fasten off.

Break yarn, leaving approximately a 6in (15cm) tail.

Legs (make 2)

Round 1: Using A, create a slip knot, ch 2.

Round 2: 6 dc into first ch.

Round 3: 2 dc into each dc (12 sts).

Round 4: Dc around.

Fasten off.

Break yarn, leaving approximately a 6in (15cm) tail.

Feet (make 2)

Round 1: Using A, create a slip knot, ch 2.

Round 2: 6 dc into first ch.

Round 3: 2 dc into each dc, (12 sts).

Fasten off.

Break yarn, leaving approximately a 6in (15cm) tail.

Making up

Using the yarn tails attached to the separate pieces, stitch the legs on first, then the feet, finishing with the eyes on top of the head, with mattress stitch (see page 140). Using the embroidery thread and backstitch (see page 140), embroider the mouth. Stitch on the seed beads for the eyes (see page 142). Push any remaining yarn tails through the body, and trim.

Who do you love enough to give your heart to? If you make some of these mini hearts you can spread your love to all your friends and family, who will adore this little keepsake.

Love heart

Finished size

Approx. ¾ x 1in (2 x 2.5cm)

Materials

Anchor Pearl Cotton No 8, 100% cotton
   (89yd/81m per 10g ball)
1 x 10g ball of 46 red (A)
1.00mm (UK4:US10) crochet hook
Toy stuffing
Large sewing needle

Heart

Top of heart is made in 2 parts.

Part 1

Round 1: Using A, create a slip knot, ch 2.

Round 2: 6 dc into first ch.

Round 3: 2 dc into each dc (12 sts).

Rounds 4–5: Dc in each dc.

Fasten off.

Part 2

Round 1: Using A, create a slip knot, ch 2.

Round 2: 6 dc into first ch.

Round 3: 2 dc into each dc (12 sts).

Rounds 4–5: Dc in each dc.

Do not fasten off this time.

Continue with part 2.

Round 6: Dc in next 9 dc.

Join to any dc on part 1 with a dc, dc in next 23 dc, place marker. (You should be at the middle of the heart.)

Rounds 7–8: Dc in each dc to marker (24 sts).

Round 9: (1 dc in next dc, dc2tog), rep to marker (16 sts).

Round 10: (Dc in next 2 dc, dc2tog), rep to marker (12 sts).

Round 11: (1 dc in next dc, dc2tog), rep to marker (8 sts).

Stuff item.

Round 12: Dc2tog around until the hole is closed. This can get tricky.

Fasten off.

Break yarn, leaving approximately a 6in (15cm) tail.

Making up

Thread the yarn tail through a large sewing needle. Close any gap left at the top then thread the remainder through the body of the heart, and trim.

> ## Tip
> *For a touch of glitz and glamour, why not stitch some tiny seed beads onto your heart charms?*

These sweet babies were made to place in my own dolls' house, but they are also perfect gift charms for new babies. So if you have a new arrival on its way to your family or friends, why not have a go at making one?

Baby bunting

Finished size

Approx. 1½ x ¾in (4 x 2cm)

Materials

Anchor Pearl Cotton No 8, 100% cotton
   (89yd/81m per 10g ball)
1 x 10g ball of 128 blue, or 48 pink (A)
1 x 10g ball of 1011 skin colour (B)
1.00mm (UK4:US10) crochet hook
Toy stuffing
Large sewing needle
Blue embroidery thread

Pink embroidery thread
Embroidery needle
Blue or pink sequin
Blue or pink seed bead
2 pearl seed beads
Beading needle
Approx. 8in (20cm) length of ⅛in (2mm) lilac
   or pink silk ribbon

Body

Round 1: Using A, create a slip knot, ch 2.

Round 2: 6 dc into first ch.

Round 3: 2 dc into each dc (12 sts).

Round 4: (1 dc in next dc, dc2inc), rep 6 times, place marker (18 sts).

Round 5: Dc around to marker.

Round 6: (1 dc in next 2 dc, dc2inc), rep around to marker (24 sts).

Rounds 7–12: Dc around to marker.

Round 13: (Dc in next 2 dc, dc2tog), rep to marker (18 sts).

Round 14: Dc around to marker.

Round 15: (1 dc in next dc, dc2tog), rep to marker (12 sts).

Stuff item.

Round 16: Dc2tog around until only a small hole is left.

Fasten off.

Break yarn, leaving approximately a 6in (15cm) tail.

Head

Round 1: Using B (this will be the front of the face), create a slip knot, ch 2.

Round 2: 6 dc into first ch.

Round 3: 2 dc into each dc (12 sts).

Round 4: (1 dc in next dc, dc2inc), rep 6 times, place marker (18 sts).

Round 5: Dc around to marker. Change to A.

Rounds 6–7: Dc around to marker.

Round 8: (Dc in next 2 dc, dc2inc) to marker (24 sts).

Round 9: Dc around to marker.

Round 10: (Dc in next 2 dc, dc2tog), rep to marker (18 sts).

Round 11: (1 dc in next dc, dc2tog), rep to marker (12 sts).

Round 12: Dc around to marker. Stuff item.

Round 13: Dc2tog around until the hole is closed.

Fasten off.

Break yarn, leaving approximately a 6in (15cm) tail.

Thread the yarn tail through a large sewing needle. Close any gap left at the top then thread the remainder through the body of the doll, and trim.

Frill

Using A, make slip knot, ch 12.

Row 1: Turn, ch 2, 2 tr into 3rd ch, (1 dc in next 2 ch, 3 tr in next ch), rep until ch completed.

Fasten off.

Making up

Using the yarn tails attached to the separate pieces, stitch the doll together with mattress stitch (see page 140). Using the blue embroidery thread and backstitch (see page 140), embroider the eyes. Using pink or blue embroidery thread, stitch the matching colour sequin to the front of the face, using the seed bead to anchor it (see page 142). Stitch the frill to the head with matching embroidery thread. Tie the ribbon around the neck, then stitch on the pearl seed beads for buttons.

As these chicks are so small they are great for many applications in jewellery, from charms, pendants and brooches to pretty earrings. So why not make yourself a complete set?

Cheeky chicks

Finished size

Approx. ¾ x ¾in (1.5 x 1.5cm)

Materials

Anchor Pearl Cotton No 8, 100% cotton
  (89yd/81m per 10g ball)
1 x 10g ball of 305 yellow (A)
1 x 10g ball of 303 orange (B)
1.00mm (UK4:US10) crochet hook
Toy stuffing
Large sewing needle
Black embroidery thread
Embroidery needle

Body

Round 1: Using A, create a slip knot, ch 2.

Round 2: 6 dc into first ch.

Round 3: 2 dc into each dc, place marker (12 sts).

Rounds 4–8: Dc around to marker.

Round 9: (Dc in next 2 dc, dc2tog), rep to marker (9 sts).

Round 10: Dc around to marker. Stuff item.

Round 11: Dc2tog around until the hole is closed.

Fasten off.

Break yarn, leaving approximately a 6in (15cm) tail.

Thread the yarn tail through a large sewing needle. Close any gap left at the top then thread the remainder through the body of the chick, and trim.

Wings (make 2)

Round 1: Using A, create a slip knot, ch 2.

Round 2: 6 dc into first ch.

Round 3: 2 dc into each dc (12 sts). Fasten off.

Break yarn, leaving approximately a 6in (15cm) tail.

Feet (make 2)

Round 1: Using B, create a slip knot, ch 2.

Round 2: 6 dc into first ch. Fasten off.

Break yarn, leaving approximately a 6in (15cm) tail.

Making up

Using the yarn tails attached to the separate pieces, stitch the wings and feet into place with mattress stitch (see page 140). Embroider the beak using shade B, by making two French knots on top of each other so they stick out (see page 141). Using the black embroidery thread and backstitch (see page 140), embroider on the eyes. Push any remaining yarn tails through the body, and trim.

Tip

You might find it easier to join the two feet together before you attach them to the body.

If you want a bit more of a challenge, then this pattern
is an ideal one to try. This little ballerina will pirouette
to centre stage and leap into your heart.

Prima ballerina

Finished size

Approx. 1½ × 1¼ in (4 × 3cm)

Materials

Anchor Pearl Cotton No 8, 100% cotton
   (89yd/81m per 10g ball)
1 × 10g ball of 1 white (A)
1 × 10g ball of 358 brown (B)
1 × 10g ball of 1011 skin colour (C)
1 × 10g ball of 52 pink (D)
1.00mm (UK4:US10) crochet hook

Toy stuffing
Large sewing needle
Blue embroidery thread
Pink embroidery thread
18 gold seed beads
Gold or yellow sewing or embroidery cotton
Beading needle

Body

Round 1: Using A, create a slip knot, ch 2.

Round 2: 6 dc into first ch.

Round 3: 2 dc into each dc (12 sts).

Round 4: (1 dc in next dc, dc2inc), rep 6 times, place marker (18 sts).

Round 5: Dc around to marker.

Round 6: (Dc in next 2 dc, dc2inc), rep around to marker (24 sts).

Rounds 7–11: Dc around to marker.

Round 12: (Dc in next 2 dc, dc2tog), rep to marker (18 sts).

Round 13: Dc around to marker.

Round 14: (1 dc in next dc, dc2tog), rep to marker (12 sts).

Rounds 15–16: Dc around to marker. Stuff item.

Round 17: Dc2tog around until only a small hole is left.

Fasten off.

Break yarn, leaving approximately a 6in (15cm) tail.

Head

Round 1: Using B, create a slip knot, ch 2.

Round 2: 6 dc into first ch.

Round 3: 2 dc into each dc, place marker (12 sts).

Round 4: (1 dc in next dc, dc2inc), rep 6 times (18 sts).

Rounds 5–6: Dc around to marker.

Round 7: (Dc in next 2 dc, dc2inc), rep to marker (24 sts).

Change to C.

Rounds 8–9: Dc around to marker.

Round 10: (Dc in next 2 dc, dc2tog), rep to marker (18 sts).

Stuff item.

Round 11: Dc2tog around until only a small hole is left.

Fasten off.

Break yarn, leaving approximately a 6in (15cm) tail.

Hair bun

Round 1: Using B, create a slip knot, ch 2.

Round 2: 6 dc into first ch.

Round 3: 2 dc into each dc (12 sts).

Fasten off.

Break yarn, leaving approximately a 6in (15cm) tail.

Skirt

Using D, ch 20.

Row 1: Turn, ch 2, 2 tr into 3rd ch from hook, 1 ch, (3 tr into next ch, 1 ch), repeat along ch.

Fasten off.

You need to watch your tension as this can make the skirt either longer or shorter.

Making up

Using the yarn tails attached to the separate pieces, stitch the doll together with mattress stitch (see page 140). Using blue embroidery thread and backstitch (see page 140), embroider the eyes; using the pink thread, embroider the mouth and dress details. Stitch the skirt on using mattress stitch, and stitch on about 16 beads for the tiara and two for the earrings (see page 142). Push any remaining yarn tails through the body, and trim.

If you love cats as much as I do then you will enjoy making these little characters. Make them in the colours of your own beloved pets. These three adorable kittens are the same colours as my own cats.

Three little kittens

Finished size
Approx. 1 x 1in (2.5 x 2.5cm)

Materials
Anchor Pearl Cotton No 8, 100% cotton
  (89yd/81m per 10g ball)
1 x 10g ball of each main colour (A)
(The colour options shown are 403 black, 398 grey
  and 1220 variegated orange)
1.00mm (UK4:US10) crochet hook

Toy stuffing
Large sewing needle
Black embroidery thread
Green embroidery thread
Embroidery needle

Body

Round 1: Using A, create a slip knot, ch 2.

Round 2: 6 dc into first ch.

Round 3: 2 dc into each st (12 sts).

Round 4: 2 dc into each st (24 sts).

Round 5: (1 dc in next dc, dc2inc), rep around, place marker (36 sts).

Rounds 6–9: Dc around.

Round 10: (Dc in next 2 dc, dc2tog), rep to marker (27 sts).

Round 11: (1 dc in next dc, dc2tog), rep to marker (18 sts).

Rounds 12–14: Dc around to marker.

Round 15: (1 dc in next dc, dc2tog) to marker (12 sts).

Stuff item.

Round 16: Dc2tog around until the hole is closed.

Fasten off.

Break yarn, leaving approximately a 6in (15cm) tail.

Thread the yarn tail through a large sewing needle. Close any gap left at the top then thread the remainder through the body of the kitten, and trim.

Ears (make 2)

Round 1: Using A, create a slip knot, ch 4.

Round 2: Turn work, dc into 2nd ch from hook, dc into 3rd ch.

Round 3: Turn work and dc2tog. Fasten off.

Break yarn, leaving approximately a 6in (15cm) tail.

Tail

Row 1: Using A, create a slip knot, ch 10.

Row 2: Turn work, dc into each ch. Fasten off.

Break yarn leaving approximately a 6in (15cm) tail.

Making up

Using the yarn tails attached to the separate pieces, stitch the ears and tail into place with mattress stitch (see page 140). Using black embroidery thread and backstitch (see page 140), embroider the nose and whiskers; using the green thread, embroider the eyes. I have left my whiskers loose to give another dimension, but they can be stitched on if preferred. Push any remaining tails through the body of the cat, and trim.

This wise old owl makes the perfect gift for bookworms and bird lovers. He will pass on his vast knowledge of everything to all who make him. Why not make him into an eye-catching bookmark charm?

Wise owl

Finished size
Approx. ¾ x 1in (2 x 2.5cm)

Materials
Anchor Pearl Cotton No 8, 100% cotton
  (89yd/81m per 10g ball)
1 x 10g ball of 46 brown (A)
1 x 10g ball of 313 orange (B)
1.00mm (UK4:US10) crochet hook

Toy stuffing
Large sewing needle
Black embroidery thread
Embroidery needle
2 black seed beads
Beading needle

Body

Round 1: Using A, create a slip knot, ch 2.

Round 2: 6 dc into first ch.

Round 3: 2 dc into each st (12 sts).

Round 4: 2 dc into each st, place marker (24 sts).

Round 5: (Dc in next 2 dc, dc2inc), rep around to marker (32 sts).

Rounds 6–12: Dc around to marker.

Round 13: (Dc in next 2 dc, dc2tog), rep to marker (24 sts).

Round 14: (Dc in next 2 dc, dc2tog), rep to marker (18 sts).

Round 15: (1 dc in next dc, dc2tog), rep to marker (12 sts).

Stuff item.

Round 16: Dc2tog around until the hole is closed.

Fasten off.

Break yarn, leaving approximately a 6in (15cm) tail.

Thread the yarn tail through a large sewing needle. Close any gap left at the top then thread the remainder through the body of the owl, and trim.

Wings (make 2)

Round 1: Using A, create a slip knot, ch 2.

Round 2: 6 dc into first ch.

Round 3: 2 dc into each st (12 sts). Fasten off.

Break yarn, leaving approximately a 6in (15cm) tail.

Feet (make 2)

Round 1: Using B, create a slip knot, ch 2.

Round 2: 6 dc into first ch. Fasten off.

Break yarn, leaving approximately a 6in (15cm) tail.

Eye rims (make 2)

Round 1: Using B, create a slip knot, ch 2.

Round 2: 6 dc into first ch. Fasten off.

Break yarn, leaving approximately a 6in (15cm) tail.

Making up

Using the yarn tails attached to the separate pieces, stitch the wings, feet and eye rims into place with mattress stitch (see page 140). Embroider the beak using shade B, by making two French knots on top of each other so they stick out (see page 141). Stitch the seed beads into the centre of the eye rims (see page 142). Push any remaining yarn tails through the body of the owl, and trim.

Some people think pumpkins should be scary, but I prefer
to see a cute grin on the face of this little pumpkin.
You can embroider any expression you want, of course.

Pumpkin Pete

Finished size

Approx. 1 x 1in (2.5 x 2.5cm)

Materials

Anchor Pearl Cotton No 8, 100% cotton
   (89yd/81m per 10g ball)
1 x 10g ball of 303 orange (A)
1 x 10g ball of 255 green (B)
1 x 10g ball in 358 brown (C)
1.00mm (UK4:US10) crochet hook

Toy stuffing
Large sewing needle
Black embroidery thread
Embroidery needle
2 black seed beads
Beading needle

Body

Round 1: Using A, create a slip knot, ch 2.

Round 2: 6 dc into first ch.

Round 3: 2 dc into each dc (12 sts).

Round 4: 2 dc into each dc, place marker (24 sts).

Round 5: (Dc in next 2 dc, dc2inc), rep 8 times (32 sts).

Rounds 6–12: Dc around to marker.

Round 13: (Dc in next 2 dc, dc2tog), rep 8 times (24 sts).

Round 14: Dc around to marker.

Round 15: (1 dc in next dc, dc2tog), rep 8 times (16 sts).

Stuff item.

Round 16 onwards: Dc2tog around until the hole is closed.

Fasten off.

Break yarn, leaving approximately a 6in (15cm) tail.

Thread the yarn tail through a large sewing needle. Close any gap left at the top then thread the remainder through the body of the pumpkin, and trim.

Leaf

Round 1: Using B, create a slip knot, ch 2.

Round 2: 6 dc into first ch.

Round 3: 2 dc into each dc (12 sts). Fasten off.

Break yarn, leaving approximately a 6in (15cm) tail.

Stalk

Round 1: Using C, create a slip knot, ch 2.

Round 2: 6 dc into first ch.

Round 3: Dc in each 6 dc.

Fasten off.

Break yarn, leaving approximately a 6in (15cm) tail.

Shape stalk over the end of the hook, turning it right side out.

Making up

Using the yarn tails attached to the separate pieces, stitch the leaf and stalk into place with mattress stitch (see page 140). Using the embroidery thread and backstitch (see page 140), embroider the face details. Stitch on the seed beads for the eyes (see page 142). Push any remaining yarn tails through the body, and trim.

With his chirpy song and plump red breast, the robin is a familiar friend to many people. So hopefully you will fall in love with this little guy and welcome him into your home.

Robin redbreast

Finished size
Approx. 1 x 1in (2.5 x 2.5cm)

Materials
Anchor Pearl Cotton No 8, 100% cotton
   (89yd/81m per 10g ball)
1 x 10g ball of 358 brown (A)
1 x 10g ball of 46 red (B)
1 x 10g ball of 303 orange (C)
1.00mm (UK4:US10) crochet hook

Toy stuffing
Large sewing needle
Blue embroidery thread
Embroidery needle

Body

Round 1: Using A, create a slip knot, ch 2.

Round 2: 6 dc into first ch.

Round 3: 2 dc into each dc (12 sts).

Round 4: 2 dc into each dc, place marker (24 sts).

Round 5: (Dc in next 2 dc, dc2inc), rep around to marker (32 sts).

Rounds 6–12: Dc around to marker.

Round 13: (Dc in next 2 dc, dc2tog), rep to marker (24 sts).

Round 14: (1 dc in next dc, dc2tog), rep to marker (16 sts).

Round 15: Dc around to marker. Stuff item.

Round 16 onwards: Dc2tog around until the hole is closed.
Fasten off.
Break yarn, leaving approximately a 6in (15cm) tail.
Thread the yarn tail through a large sewing needle. Close any gap left at the top then thread the remainder through the body of the robin, and trim.

Chest

Round 1: Using B, create a slip knot, ch 2.

Round 2: 6 dc into first ch.

Round 3: 2 dc into each dc (12 sts).

Round 4: 2 dc into each dc (24 sts).
Fasten off.
Break yarn, leaving approximately a 6in (15cm) tail.

Wings (make 2)

Round 1: Using A, create a slip knot, ch 2.

Round 2: 6 dc into first ch.

Round 3: 2 dc into each dc (12 sts).
Fasten off.
Break yarn, leaving approximately a 6in (15cm) tail.

Feet (make 2)

Round 1: Using C, create a slip knot, ch 2.

Round 2: 6 dc into first ch.
Fasten off.
Break yarn, leaving approximately a 6in (15cm) tail.

Making up

Using the yarn tails attached to the separate pieces, stitch the chest, wings and feet into place with mattress stitch (see page 140). Embroider the beak using shade C, by making two French knots on top of each other so they stick out (see page 141). Using the blue embroidery thread and backstitch (see page 140), embroider the eyes. Push any remaining yarn tails through the body, and trim.

Techniques

Getting started

To create these projects, only a limited amount of equipment is required, but it is important that you get the correct products.

Safety warning

These miniature characters are designed to be used as charms and jewellery components and are not intended to be toys. Be aware that young children could choke on these small items and their attached parts, such as beads and chains.

Scale

The patterns are not exclusive to mini-makes; just by altering the yarn thickness and by moving up a hook size you will get a larger version (see pages 134–5).

Yarn

For all the projects, I have used Anchor Pearl Cotton No 8.

You will, of course, only use small amounts, so try to choose colours that you could perhaps make other items from. It is not possible to give accurate amounts of yarn when you are working at such a small scale, but the 10g ball suggested for the patterns should give you enough to get several items from one ball.

Other yarns are available, such as DMC 80 crochet cotton, but your scale will vary slightly.

Hooks

There are a variety of crochet hooks available; including metal, bamboo and even ergonomically designed ones for comfort, but for this scale the choice becomes limited and the metal/steel hooks seem to be the predominant ones. Some of the small-scale hooks have gold-plated tips, which can help with easing the hook through the yarn.

For the projects in the book, I have kept to a 1.00mm (UK4:US10) hook, so it is not too small if you are new to making miniatures.

It is essential to keep your hooks clean, as over time they can become sticky or greasy. The simplest way is to wash them in warm water that contains a small amount of detergent and then make sure you rinse and dry them thoroughly.

Needles

For sewing up work, I find a
tapestry needle works best, but
as long as the needle has an eye
large enough for the yarn and a
sharp point then any will work.
The sharp point works better,
as with miniatures it can sometimes
be difficult to push through the yarn.
Just be careful with your fingers.

I also use a beading needle for sewing
on the seed beads and sequins; take
care with them as they bend easily.

Clean workspace and hands

I have already mentioned clean hooks, but it is just as important to
keep your hands clean as natural oils can easily be transferred to the
yarn. A good tip is to keep the ball in a small plastic snap-top bag, fastened
just enough for the yarn to run through. This not only keeps the yarn
clean, but stops it from running around the room.

Tweezers

An odd item, you may think, but for
stuffing small items tweezers can be
very helpful for picking up and pushing
the stuffing into tricky areas.

Working in a small scale

Sometimes, particularly if you are not used to working in small scale, the size of these projects can frighten some people away. In my class, the students start with larger-sized pieces and then are slowly introduced to the smaller hooks and finer cotton. This is usually the best way to start when you have not created any miniature items before.

The patterns mainly stay the same and it is only the hook and yarn size that make the difference, although the tension that you crochet at can also play a part.

I have included some examples of how the same pattern from one of the projects in this book can be made larger.

This is a great way to get the most from the book and a way to practise if you have not worked this small before.

Large-scale cupcake using a 6.00mm hook and chunky yarn.

All items are shown actual size

6.00mm   4.00mm   2.00mm   1.00mm

2

Medium-scale cupcake using
a 4.00mm hook and DK yarn.

3

Small-scale cupcake using a 2.00mm
hook and 4-ply yarn.

4

Miniature cupcake using a 1.00mm hook
and Anchor Pearl cotton No 8.

Crochet techniques

Here, we introduce some of the basic techniques that are the building blocks of crochet work and can be practised to improve your skills.

Holding the hook

The most common holding positions for the crochet hook are the 'pen' hold or the 'knife'.

Personally, I don't think that there is a right or wrong way to hold the hook. As a teacher, I have seen people using many different methods including left-handed students who use a completely different position. The only issue is tension, but as long as you keep your yarn running smoothly and your tension is even, that is all that matters.

I have had students spending far too much time worrying about this rather than enjoying their crochet. My best advice is to try the traditional methods and adjust to what feels comfortable for you. I prefer to have my index finger raised and hold the work with my thumb and middle finger.

Slip knot

This is a simple but important little knot. Leaving a long end of yarn, make a loop, then take the other end of yarn around the back of the loop and pull through. Place the loop on your hook. The knot should have some movement and not be too tight.

Making a chain

A chain is a common feature of most crochet work and usually one of the first techniques a beginner will learn.

I

2

3

I Make a slip knot and put the yarn over the hook. Do not tighten up the slip knot too much or you will not be able to pull the hooked yarn through.

2 Pull the loop of the knot through. You now have your first chain.

3 Repeat this until you have the desired number of chains.

Double crochet

I Push the hook through either the next stitch or chain. Hook yarn then pull through. Pull the yarn through, giving you two loops on the hook.

2 Hook the yarn again and pull through both loops. Repeat this until you have the required length.

I

2

Treble crochet

Treble crochet is only used a few times in this book, but it creates a lovely effect.

1 Put the yarn over the hook. Push the hook through the chosen stitch or chain. Hook the yarn around and pull through, giving you three loops on the hook.

2 Hook yarn and pull through two loops.

3 Hook yarn and pull through remaining two loops.

4 One loop left on hook. Repeat as needed.

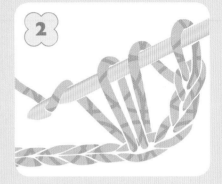

Decreasing
(dc2tog)

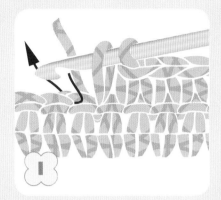 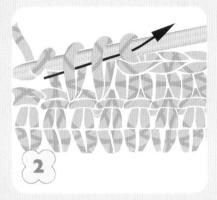 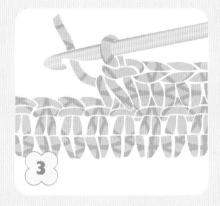

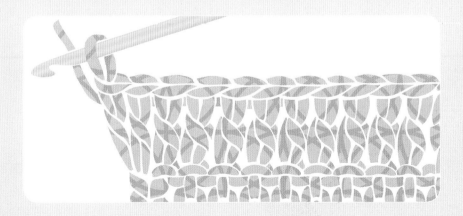

1 Push the hook through the next stitch or chain. Hook yarn and pull through, giving you two loops on the hook. Push the hook through the next stitch or chain. Hook the yarn and pull through.

2 You now have three loops on the hook. Hook the yarn and pull through these three loops.

3 There is now one loop left on the hook.

Increasing
(dc2inc)

Increasing stitches couldn't be simpler; all you have to do is complete two double crochet stitches into the same stitch below.

Finishing touches

Here we outline the techniques you will need to make up your Amigurumi, as well as giving you some ideas on how to embellish your characters.

Fastening off your work

When fastening off your work, leave a nice long thread, so it can be used to attach other parts. When it is no longer required, push the thread through the body of the item and then trim off any excess.

Mattress stitch

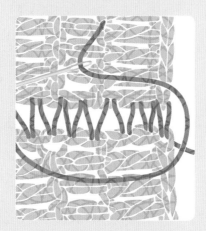

This simple method is used when joining two separate pieces together.

Using the long thread tails, pick up a stitch close to the edge of one side, pulling the two edges close. Push the needle through the opposite side and repeat until the area required is neatly closed.

Backstitch

I have used this method for most embellishments on the projects in this book.

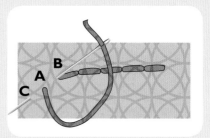

1 First bring the thread through at point **A**.

2 Take the thread back through into **B**.

3 Finally, bring the thread back up through **C**. Repeat as required.

French knots

1 After pulling the needle and thread through to the position required, wrap the thread twice around the needle.

2 Carefully push the needle back through the same hole it came from.

For the bird projects I have repeated this into the same space until the beak stands proud.

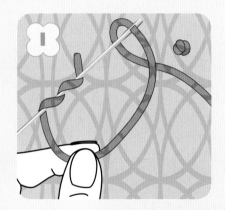

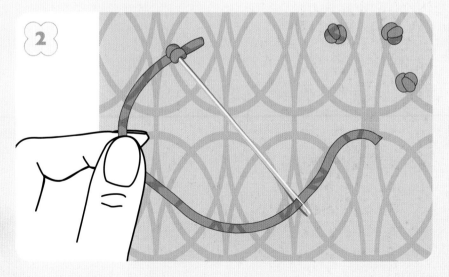

Attaching seed beads

Adding beads to your work can really make the project stand out. It is a simple process but can take a little time.

1 Take a good-quality beading needle and thread with the required length of sewing cotton or one strand of embroidery thread. Make a small knot at the end and thread through at the required position on your project. Try to hide the knot as much as possible.

2 After pulling the thread completely through, thread a bead onto the needle.

3 Now push the needle back through the item, leaving a small gap from the entrance position.

4 Push the needle back through the item to the required position and continue. If you want your bead to be extra secure, push back through the bead for a second time.

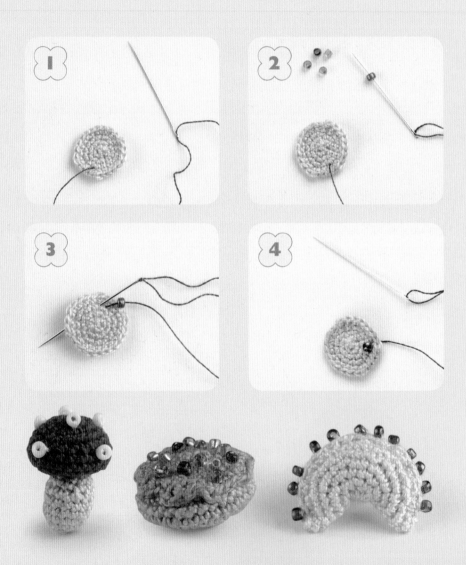

Creating loops

This is a simple method and is used to create the lion's mane.

1 Thread an embroidery needle with embroidery thread or cotton, making a knot at the end. Using a few strands of embroidery thread will make a thicker loop than just one strand on its own. Push through the item where you wish to start.

2 Allowing a loop to form, push the needle back in again, leaving only a tiny gap between stitches.

3 Continue in this way until the area required is covered.

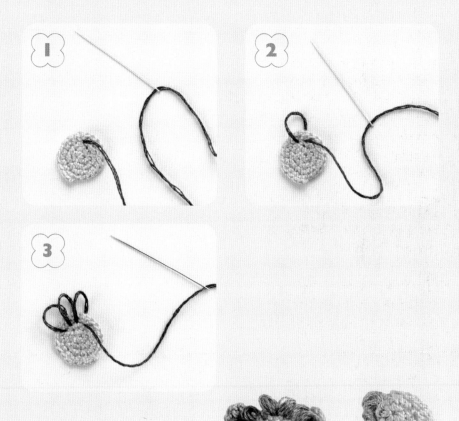

Adding tufts

This technique is used to make tufts such as the ones used on the bird's head and the pony's mane.

1 Take a length of embroidery thread and fold it in half. Thread both ends through an embroidery needle. Push the needle through and out of the desired area, leaving a tiny gap between stitches (the closer the better). Don't pull it completely through the item.

2 Take the needle out and thread the two loose ends through the loop that has formed at the back.

3 Pull tight to create your first tuft and trim to the right length. Continue in this way until you have enough tufts.

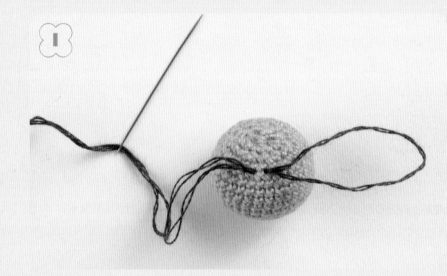

Adding legs and antennae

Add legs and antennae to characters such as the butterfly and bee using this simple technique.

1 Thread a needle with a length of embroidery thread or your yarn. Push through and out of the desired area, leaving a tiny gap between stitches (the closer the better).

2 Remove the needle and knot the two pieces together close to the body to fix into place.

3 Trim to the length required for legs or antennae.

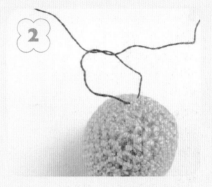

Using your mini Amigurumi

Now it's up to you! There are lots of ways you can use your creations; the only boundary is your own imagination. Here are some ideas that I hope you will like and that will inspire you.

Bracelets

Use a standard charm bracelet that can be obtained from many craft or jewellery-making shops. Attach the mini Amigurumi, some beads of your choice and any other charms with jumprings (see page 149), alternating the items to create the desired effect.

Earrings

Attach a jumpring to your items (see page 149). Then, using a second jumpring, attach the earring hook. If you like, you could lengthen the earrings using beads between the jumprings.

Bookmarks

Bookmark crooks are readily available and make a great gift for any book-loving friends. Attach a jumpring to your mini Amigurumi (see page 149), then, using a second jumpring, attach a crook, in the same way as you did for the earrings. You could add an extra string of beads if you like, in a favourite colour.

Charms and keyrings

Add some beads to your creations using jumpring attachments (see page 149) and jewellery head and eye pins. When everything is made that you require, attach the items securely to a keyring attachment.

Pendants

Use a head pin to push through the mini Amigurumi and create a loop (see page 150). Add a jumpring (see page 149), and then attach to the ribbon. You can also use some chain, cord or leather thong if you prefer.

Brooches

I have made many of these and they couldn't be simpler. All you need is a brooch back attachment, which can be obtained from many craft or jewellery-making shops. Any of the projects can become a simple brooch with a few secure stitches (see page 151).

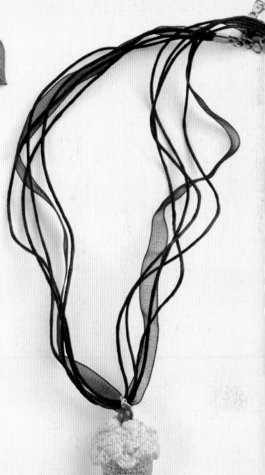

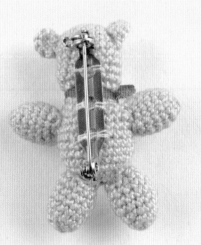

Basic jewellery techniques

To turn your completed mini Amigurumi projects into lovely gifts or jewellery pieces, some basic equipment and simple techniques are required.

Equipment and materials

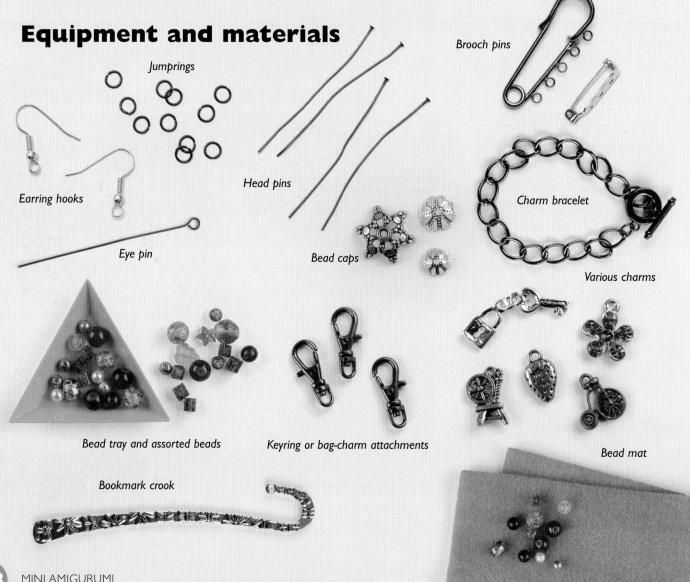

Jumprings

Brooch pins

Earring hooks

Head pins

Eye pin

Bead caps

Charm bracelet

Various charms

Bead tray and assorted beads

Keyring or bag-charm attachments

Bead mat

Bookmark crook

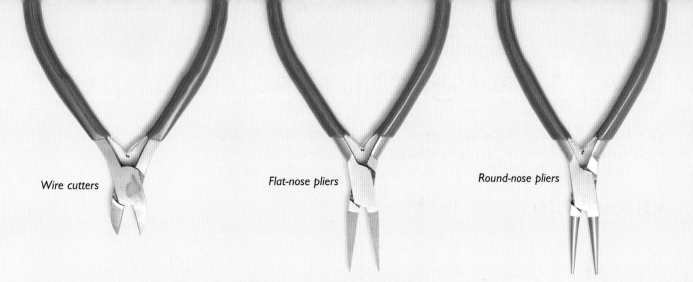

Wire cutters · Flat-nose pliers · Round-nose pliers

Opening and closing a jumpring

This is a simple but important technique. It is very easy to make the jumpring too elongated, have the edges overlap when closed, or even for them to become completely squashed or broken. But if you follow this method, you should get a perfect jumpring every time.

1 Use two pairs of flat-nose pliers; others can be used but I find these easier. Hold each end of the jumpring with a set of pliers, with the opening at the top. Gently move the pliers in opposite directions. Try not to be too heavy-handed.

2 To close the jumpring, the method is reversed until the opening meets. It may take a little practice, but it is quite easy.

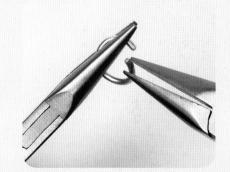

Attaching jumprings

Jumprings are attached to mini Amigurumi in the following way. Push a tapestry needle through the crochet stitches in the area you want the jumpring to sit. Then push an opened jumpring through the hole you have created, trying not to split the stitches. Carefully close the jumpring again.

Making a loop on a head or eye pin

1 After adding your bead(s), cut the pin to leave approximately ¼in (6mm) of wire. Be careful when cutting, as the wire sometimes shoots off in odd directions.

2 Using round-nose pliers, bend the wire at the angle shown. Curl the wire around the pliers to make a loop.

3 You should have a neat loop at the end of your wire.

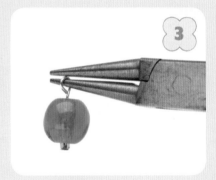

Stitching on a brooch back

1 Using strong cotton (contrast colour used here for clarity), stitch through the holes and over the sides of the brooch back, and then fasten off.

Conversions

Miniature hooks

Metric (mm)	Old UK	US
0.60	6	14
–	5½	13
0.75	5	12
–	4½	11
1.00	4	10
–	3½	9
1.25	3	8
1.50	2½	7
1.75	2	6
–	1½	5

Standard hooks

Metric (mm)	Old UK	US
2.00	14	–
2.25	13	B/1
2.50	12	–
2.75	–	C/2
3.00	11	–
3.25	10	D/3
3.50	9	E/4
3.75	–	F/5
4.00	8	G/6

Abbreviations

ch	chain
dc	double crochet
dc2inc	2 double crochet stitches in 1 stitch (increasing)
dc2tog	double crochet two stitches together (decreasing)
rep	repeat
st(s)	stitch(es)
ss	slip stitch
tr	treble crochet

UK/US crochet terms

UK	US
Double crochet	Single crochet
Half treble	Half double crochet
Treble	Double crochet
Double treble	Triple crochet
Treble treble	Double triple crochet

About the author

Sara Scales began crafting at an early age in many different mediums. Over the years, this developed into a fascination with anything small-scale and she began to explore the exciting world of miniatures – specializing in cross stitch, felting, beading and teddy-bear making. Having taught herself how to crochet and then developing an interest in the Japanese art of Amigurumi, it was a natural progression for Sara to begin scaling them down. She is a regular contributor to *The Dolls' House Magazine*, and sells her work through shops, fairs and etsy.com. She keeps a craft blog (minidreamz. blogspot.com) and teaches crochet to classes of all abilities. Sara lives with her family, two cats and a dog in a small village in South Yorkshire, England.

Acknowledgements

Firstly, I would like to thank the amazing team at GMC Publications who have been patient, supportive and encouraging throughout the whole process, and have guided me step-by-step – making this an exciting and enjoyable experience. Also, I would like to thank Geoff Briggs from Sign Posts, without whom I never would have had the confidence to pursue my dreams in the first place. Julie Bradwell, my business partner, who gave me the final push to send the e-mail that resulted in this publication and also for her continued support. My mum, Helen Leigh, without whom I would not have the passion or skills for crafting – she has been both my inspiration and my teacher. Last, but not least, thank you to my husband Shaun, my children Charlotte and Thomas, my friend Dawn Ding who will be ready to celebrate with me and to all my crochet students and shop visitors who have supported me.

Index

Project names are shown in *italics*

To place an order, or to request a catalogue, contact:

GMC Publications Ltd

Castle Place, 166 High Street, Lewes, East Sussex, BN7 1XU

United Kingdom

Tel: +44 (0)1273 488005

www.gmcbooks.com